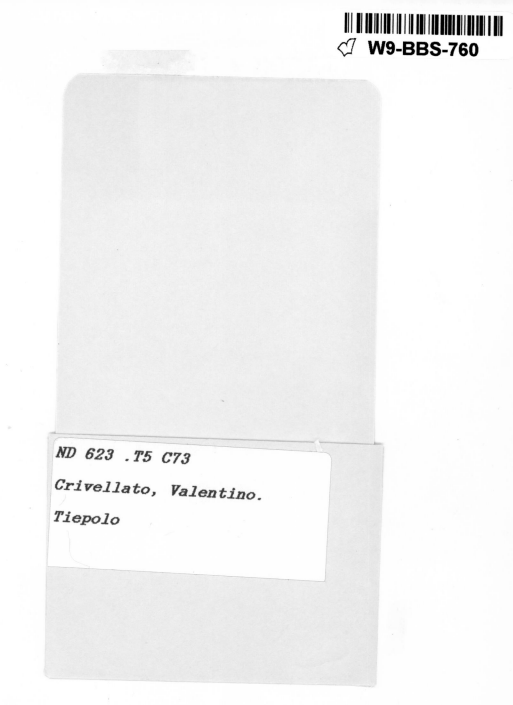

TIEPOLO

MASTERS AND MOVEMENTS

VALENTINO CRIVELLATO

Translated from the Italian by ANTHONY RHODES

TIEPOLO

W. W. NORTON & COMPANY INC
NEW YORK

28871

In 1715, when Giambattista Tiepolo received his first commission, he was aged nineteen. From then, until his death in 1770, his creative production, either in his native city, Venice, or during his many journeys in the rest of Italy and abroad, continued with scarcely a break — a long working period of more than half a century. Udine, Milan, Vicenza, Bergamo, Verona, — he travelled everywhere from the city of the lagoons, crossing the Alps twice, once to Würzburg in Franconia, and once to work at the Royal Court in Madrid. His work was known throughout Europe, and he decorated the royal palaces of Bavaria, Franconia, Prussia, Saxony, Spain and Russia. Apart from the last two decades of his life, when he was helped by his sons Giandomenico and Lorenzo, he worked almost exclusively on his own, with tireless energy, and with remarkable spontaneity and speed. As early as 1726, when he was only thirty, he is described in a written agreement with a client as 'famous'.

He painted all subjects, sacred, profane, jovial, dramatic, scenes of ornate visual opulence, as well as of deep spiritual, even religious, feeling, forcing himself, sometimes almost to the detriment of his health, to discover new problems and new modes of expression. His best work was for the easel and the fresco. In the latter he excelled, for if his canvases and smaller paintings revealed that intense poetic feeling, that spontaneity and fluency, which informs all his work, it is in the great frescoes, the vast designs spread over whole walls of palaces and churches, that we see him at his best. On these great expanses, the painting seems to overflow, bursting, exploding with light and sunshine as it moves from surface to surface. Here, Tiepolo

5

surpasses all painters, past and present, in conveying an extraordinary effect of space and atmosphere. Thanks to his innate feeling for space, expressing itself in this explosion of light, producing this gay and joyful atmosphere, Tiepolo could, whenever he wished, give an illusion of all that is dazzling and intoxicating in life. There is a musical element, too, in his painting, for he could create a world of colours as a symphonist creates his harmonies, not sequence of notes and semi-tones and musical phrases, but, by some strange alchemy of his own, a chord of colours vibrating in visual shapes and forms. His genius brought the vibrating light of the sun into the nocturnal scenes of the late Baroque painters, and into the pale anaemic canvases of the *chiaristi* of the period. He dared to open up the ceilings and vaults of the churches and palaces on to the boundless sky, and here, beyond the force of gravity as it were, he placed his triumphant bands of angels and troops of dazzling women. In the originality of this discovery lies his greatest contribution to Venetian painting in the eighteenth century; and it was for this originality, together with his inexhaustible productivity, that he received the acclamation and patronage of the great, first in Venice, then in Italy, and finally throughout Europe.

Other fine painters were at work at the same time, in the halls and *stanze* of the great houses: Dorigny, Piazzetta, Sebastiano Ricci, Pellegrini, Amigoni, all well equipped to satisfy that desire for showy splendour which distinguished the taste of the aristocracy and the high clergy. Rosalba Carriera, Canaletto, Bellotto, Pietro Longhi and Francesco Guardi, were also contemporaries, but they worked in a different, a more modest, way, less concerned with pampering and idealising the great, than with depicting them as they really were. Some of these men had already achieved fame in the rest of Europe, where their work was in constant demand. But the most in demand, the most acclaimed of all by the great and the rich, was Tiepolo, who came to be regarded as the restorer of the sixteenth-century tradition. Indeed, the phrase Venetian painting soon came to mean simply Tiepolo's painting.

How shall we account for his phenomenal success? A good reason, which has been advanced, is that no one was more aware than Tiepolo that, as the Venetian nobility declined politically and economically, it sought increasingly to evoke the memory of its glorious past, and to exalt its present, with spectacular public and private displays. With the presentiment of death about it, the aristocracy of Venice lived for the moment, enjoying every possible refinement of life, surrounding itself with a flow of unending pleasure, intoxicating itself with the blandishments of imagined glory. To the great mass of cosmopolitan merchants and travellers who visited it, Venice, during most of the eighteenth century, seemed the fabulous city of this aristocracy, of perennial gaiety, of exquisite tastes and graces, offering a life of ease among festivities, gallantries, and delicious adventures of every kind. Yet this over-refined conception of life, this world of fatuous gilded idlers, was not all. Picturesquely blended with it was another world, equally active, the world of the thinkers and writers and artists, men who were less removed from the realities of the changing eighteenth century, sensitive too, and often touched by, the new ideas now fermenting in France, by the *lumière* she was diffusing throughout the world. Frequently lively and brilliant, always fertile in ideas, these literary and academic circles were served by famous printers such as Albrizi, the Pasquales, and the Zattas. They had newspapers and magazines, the *Giornale dei Letterati* in which Apostolo Zeno held forth, or the *Frusta Letteraria* edited by Baretti or the *Gazzetta* in which Gozzi wrote. Musically, too, with Benedetto Marcello and Antonio Vivaldi, Venice was one of the most important cities of Europe. While on the stage Carlo Goldoni's penetrating yet good-humoured observation of the foibles of life, inaugurated the rebirth of Italian comedy.

But the over-all tone was still set by the aristocracy, conserv-

ative, refined, good-mannered, a trifle frivolous, flaunting the tinsel
of the past, over-indulgent in the pomp of the present, rich with
the blandishments of its poets and artists, whose task was to cele-
brate the great deeds of the past and exalt those of the present.
Tiepolo, with his astonishing powers of adaptation, his vivacity and
phantasy, welcomed and interpreted all the ideals of this society,
translating them into a world of form and colour. A fitting tribute
to his powers was expressed by the Count of Tessin, the Minister
of Fine Arts to the King of Sweden, a man of exquisite taste, and
a connoisseur of painting. The King had wanted Tiepolo to work
for him, and Tessin wrote, ' This artist is a man of infinite warmth
and colour, possessed of an individual character and spirit, yet ever
ready to adapt himself, with marvellous rapidity, to any new re-
quirements... '.

We meet the painter for the first time in the workshop of Gregorio Lazzarini, a painter then in fashion among these ruling circles
who were later to receive Tiepolo with such acclaim. When still a
boy, Tiepolo helped his master mix colours and prepare canvases,
while learning design, perspective, and the composition of those figure
groups to which the seventeenth-century painters ingeniously gave
movement and life, those atmospheric scenes, softly irridescent in
a decorative and declamatory setting, painted in the clearest of colours. But he soon tired of the lifeless formalism of old Lazzarini and
left the workshop; his enthusiasm for the new and the untried, his
impulsive character, his sense of phantasy and his desire to find his
own way, forced him to examine the world around him, the entire
world of Venetian painting.

Not long before this, Fumiani had completed his paintings in
the Church of St Pantalon; even more recently, those of Dorigny
in St Silvestro and of Sebastiano Ricci in St Marziale, had been painted. Spread out before the young painter, therefore, in the *Palazzi*

PLATE I - THE EDUCATION
OF THE VIRGIN
DIGIONE MUSEUM

PLATE 2 - MARTYRDOM OF SAINT BARTHOLOMEW - CHURCH OF SAN STAE, VENICE

PLATE 3 - THE CARMELITE MADONNA. DETAIL - BRERA, MILAN ▶

PLATE 4 - TEMPTATION OF SAINT ANTONY - BRERA, MILAN

PLATE 5 - ZEFIRUS AND FLORA. DETAIL - CA' REZZONICO, VENICE ▶

PLATE 6 - SCIPIO AND THE SLAVE. DETAIL - PALAZZO DUGNANI, MILAN

PLATE 7 - MAGNANIMITY OF SCIPIO. DETAIL - PALAZZO DUGNANI, MILAN

PLATE 8 - THE ADORATION OF THE CHILD - SACRESTY OF SAN MARCO, VENICE

and churches of Venice, was the whole of seventeenth-century Venetian painting, from Fetti to Liss, from Strozzi to Mazzoni, from Maffei to Celesti. Last, and most important, there were the works of the great fathers of the Venetian school, from Titian to Tintoretto and Veronese. But the interests of the impetuous young Tiepolo went immediately to two Venetian representatives of the Bologna school of painting, headed by Crespi: Bencovic and Piazzetta. Sharing something of their force and vehemence, he was quickly attracted by their plastic, foreshortened figures, as well as by his desire to break with the anaemic academism of his master.

It was to Bencovic that he turned first, the painter of gloomy tormented visions, whose figures delineated with with broken contours and illuminated with sudden flashes of light have a flat anatomical shape. His influence on Tiepolo is clear in the *Sacrifice of Isaac* in the Ospedaletto, the first authenticated work of the young Tiepolo, painted in about 1716. It is part of a series of apostles and prophets painted in the interstices of the arches, a different artist being commissioned for each interstice. The limited space in which he had to work forced Tiepolo to compress his figures and distort them in the ' affected ' manner of Bencovic; but the daring of his light on the anguished scenes is something new. This painting is far superior to any of the others in the series.

Tiepolo's enthusiasm for Bencovic appears again in the *Rejection of Agar* in the Rasini collection in Milan (dated 1717 or 1719), especially in the nervously drawn figure of Agar, the bending movement of the old man depicted in chiaroscuro. But entirely Tiepolo's own, the revelation of a new talent with its own intense phantasy, is the sure and courageous way in which the dramatic scene is handled, the more expansive and fluent modelling, the toned-down colouring. A subtle novelty is also introduced in the two feminine faces which emerge from the shadows, scarcely touched by the light. They have a foretaste of that sweet expression we are to see later enlivening his sunny skies, on the faces of his angels and young girls, their tender eyelids half-closed.

In about 1721, we find the young artist in competition, as he had been at the Ospedaletto five years before, with the first painters of his time, Lazzarini, Balestra, Bambini, Ricci, Piazzetta, over the series of apostles to be painted as decoration for the new city church of St Stae. His *Martyrdom of St Bartholomew* (PL. 2 of the illustrations in this book) is pulsatingly alive and moving; the dramatic figure of the saint dominates the entire scene, his arms thrown wide open as he falls sideways, his body corruscating with light against the darkened background. The restlessness of the painter's youthful mind, and his anxiety to discover new pictorial solutions, inform the whole of this painting. Rather than re-echo the expressionism of Bencovic, Tiepolo prefers here to be influenced by the manner of Piazzetta, by his liveliness and luminosity, his tingling, vibrating atmosphere in *St James the Martyr* (in the same church), which he took as a model. To this new influence can be attributed the softer modelling of the figures, the more careful laying-on of colour, and the colours themselves, at once cleaner, more original and more flowing.

The example of Piazzetta helped Tiepolo to escape from the influence of Bencovic's luminous expressionism, bringing him a step nearer to his own personal language, in which there is a more harmonious combination of colour and light. Piazzetta's influence is to be seen in *Carmelite Madonna with Penitent Souls* with its solemn but well-modelled and foreshortened figures, as well as in the broad application of the paint; he painted this between 1721 and 1722 for the Church of St Aponal, and it is now in the Brera Pinacoteca in Milan. But the personal Tiepolo touch, displaying his greatest powers, is already evident in the serene and measured quality of the monumental central group, its daring perspective, and the painter's sensitive, nervous brushwork.

In the period that follows, Piazzetta's influence, which we may, more generically, call academic-realism, begins to decline. Contributing to Tiepolo's new lyrical approach was his growing interest in contemporary painters' problems concerning space and filling it with glowing luminosity, as well as an awareness that his true vocation lay with broad visions of light and space. Here, the example of Sebastiano Ricci appears to have played a decisive role. This painter had renounced his earlier plastic-baroque and was painting in a kind of neo-Veronese manner, full of superficial splendour, of formal elegance, grandiloquent gestures, coloured atmospheric effects, a style at once varied, affected and full of light, a style we may call Court-Decorative.

Quite as important as this painter for Tiepolo was Giannantonio Pellegrini, who worked mostly abroad, and whose figures seemed weightless in the air, palpitating in the luminous skies.

Between 1720 and 1725, Tiepolo worked on the fresco of the *Gloria di Santa Teresa* at the Church of the Scalzi, in the vault of a side chapel. It was his first great work of a purely decorative nature, and he set about it with his usual enthusiams. Although surrounded by other paintings characterised by a baroque heaviness, he boldly launched out his choirs of angels across the vault, seating the saint in his airy luminous skies.

His fame now began to spread and commissions came pouring in. In about 1725, we find him in the Corte dell'Albero in Venice, decorating the Palazzo Sandi, whose walls were still pungent with the smell of quicklime. He decorated its ceiling with a fresco exalting the *Force of Eloquence*, in a ιythological allegory. Combined with echoes of the baroque and his own as yet uncertain inventions, in a composition not entirely homogeneous, is his wonderful invention of a Pegasus, hurling itself with Theseus on to the Hydra. This animal is all passion and ardour, blazing with light, its great wings spread out across the sky; it is the forerunner of that great family of superb war chargers destined to burst forth in cavalcades like blazing meteors across the boundless Tiepolo skyscapes. The decoration of this room was completed with three wall canvases (now at Castelgomberto Vicentino), conceived with exceptional fluency and variety of invention, of which the largest, representing the episode of *Achilles discovered by Ulysses among the daughters of Licomede*, is notable for its novel treatment — the unconstrained composition, the new physionomies, the clothing, the dance movement of the female figures, and finally, for that delicious pictorial fragment, the young girls wearing their bright jewels, the whole scene shot through with searing light, and redolent of a kind of lingering gentleness. The rural background is now painted with his new colours, brighter, more glaring, irridescent on the silky raiments. The treatment in these paintings reveals an origin clarly unconnected with the sober popular tradition of Piazzetta, but which derives from the still lingering seventeenth century golden age of painters, the Court-Decorative or sumptuous Veronese style of which Sebastiano Ricci, with his luminous figures rustling with silk, was the fervent imitator. There is something, too, in it of the graceful musical quality of the rococo age now in fashion.

Between 1725 and 1728 Tiepolo was commissioned by the Dolfin family to decorate their Venetian palace with a series of ten large canvases, representing episodes from Roman history; and simultaneously, a member of the same family, Diogini, the patriarch of Udine, commissioned him to paint a cycle of frescoes for his *palazzo*, the Archbishop's Palace. In these scenes from Roman history, which are now dispersed all over the world (in Vienna, Leningrad, New York) Tiepolo most felicitously develops the new methods he had discovered while working in the Palazzo Sandi; ever fecund in invention, he invests his figures with even more light and sunshine. Here for the first time, in the easy lively touch, we are aware of an artist who is mature. At Udine, in the contract for the decoration of the

PLATE 9 - BAPTISM OF JESUS - CAPPELLA COLLEONI, BERGAMO

PLATE IO - THE BAPTIST PREACHING. SKETCH - COLLECTION G. TRECCANI, MILAN

PLATE II - THE BAPTIST PREACHING - CAPPELLA COLLEONI, BERGAMO

Gio: Batta. Tiepolo f.

ANGEL'S HEAD - CORRER MUSEUM, VENICE

◀ THREE NUDES - MUNICIPAL MUSEUM, UDINE

Cappella del Sacramento in the Cathedral (which was included in his fresco work for the Archbishop's Palace), he is referred to as ' the celebrated painter of luminosity '. This was in 1726 when Tiepolo was exactly thirty years old. The episodes in the Cathedral do not add however greatly to his reputation; he had to confine his work in a precipitous ribbed vault of the presbytery, on a small, poorly illuminated surface, and the choir of angels he painted have little of his usual phantasy of daring. He was probably influenced by the bravura and later baroque perspective, the foreshortened stage effects of Dorigny, the well-known decorator of the Roman school, who had painted in the same vault.

Tiepolo's most subtle originality is to be seen instead in the *stanze* of the Archbishop's Palace, in the joyful, fresh and dazzling *Story of Agar*, of Jacob, Abraham, Sarah, Rachel and Solomon. Here, provides a feast of youthfulness, of winged and curly headed cherubs, of mountain scenery and airy skies, all bathed in the bright and fiery light of his crystalline colours. Here, on the threshold of Sarah's dwelling, in the clear light of the morning, is the huge Tiepolo female angel with her outspread wings, the luscious flesh of her thighs painted in dazzling colours beneath the undulating draperies, the silver and rose reflections on her face and on the high collar, which, like some luminous aureole, is wrapped around her throat. Abraham is listening with half closed eyes, mesmerised by the whispering of three curly headed angels, illuminated by the sunny light of day which, through the curve in his arms, shines on a palpitating landscape of cypresses and houses reposing on a peaceful mountain slope. In *Rachel discovering the Idols*, Tiepolo paints the mountain alpine light falling on figures which are clearly seen in the foreground, but which diminish and weaken as the light declines, so that in the background, the objects he paints become increasingly more nebulous, until they merge into his enchanting landscape of mountains, evoked rather than drawn, in the faraway blue distance. Also in the painting, quite distinct from the main theme, is the figure of the young shepherd on the mountain top; although foreshortened, it is obviously drawn from life, with which it is pulsating.

Tiepolo had never achieved such atmospheric effects as here, a rendering so fresh, precise yet poetical, a scene in which we feel the painter is almost present himself, physically. Great as was his later work, nothing in it surpasses this relatively early picture. His new and individual treatment of sky and landscape, throwing it wide open to the air of heaven, was to remain unchanged, without any further development, at least until the last period of his working life. As we shall show, Tiepolo was too much of a virtuoso painter, and too full of phantasy, to enter into a close, affectionate relationship with nature; his aim was not so much to copy nature, nor to exalt it, as to abstract subjects from it; his gorgeous scenes frequently have a natural setting or background, but they are idealised, unreal. With their Court-Decorative overtones, after the manner of Ricci and Veronese, they seem to be part of an elaborate stage-setting. The light, too, which illuminates this stage is abstract and unreal, unconnected with the hour of the day, of the natural surroundings, a luminous light of Tiepolo's own making, timeless and boundless, a vibrating apollonian light, enabling him to transform his rich clients, or the saints they wished him to draw, to exalt them, surrounding them with the flurry of wings, and the beauty of youthful bodies. It is only in his later work that he leaves his ethereal skies and comes down for a moment to earth, in the landscapes he painted around Vicenza (at Valmarana), at Este and in Spain, where he seems aware of something tangible, something real, which he depicts with his own brand of subtle melancholy.

The list of these paintings of the first period, when Tiepolo was in his twenties, is completed by an entire series of medium-sized and small canvases, which he painted in the intervals between his larger, more important commissions, all revealing his constant search for new means of expression. They deal with a variety of subjects, mostly of a historical-mythological nature, free and lively in composition, full of colour; the human figures which people them are rendered with a rapid, nervous hand, ingeniously incorporated in the background of ever changing light. Notable among them are: *The Rape of the Sabine Women* in the Helsinki Museum, only a sketch, but vibrating with Tiepolo's lighting effects; the canvases *Diana and Atteone* and *The Rape of Europe* in the Venetian Galleries, both full of beautiful graceful figures, and gorgeous colours, set in a fabled landscape; *The Venus at the Mirror* of the Gerli Collection in Milan, a weightless lady, her rosy flesh floating on a sea of velvet. Then there is the delicious scene of the *Temptation of St Anthony* (PL. 4) in the Brera Pinakothek, spontaneous and painted as it were with the tip of the brush. The contrast of colours is particularly daring here — the white flash of a cloud above the darkened body of the saint, then to the left, with the light falling on it, the naked flesh of the woman, tremulous with sensual blandishments. *The Sacrifice of Iphigenia* in the Giustinian Collection in Venice is full of violent *chiaroscuro* among the vibrant, burning colours. In his witty painting *Alexander and Campasne in the studio of Apelles* the studio is none other than that of Tiepolo himself, and the artist has depicted himself seated in the chair of the great man, while the beautiful Campaspe is his wife, Cecilia Guardi (the sister of the painters Antonio and Francesco, and happily married to Tiepolo since 1719), and at their side he has shown their little servant Alim, with their pet pekingnese dog.

In 1731 we find Tiepolo in Milan, about to start on the hardest working year of his life. Here he decorated the Palazzi Archinto and Casati (then Dugnani), the first with frescoes on four of its ceilings (destroyed by bombardments in 1943), with subjects taken from mythology, among which is the famous *Fetonte with the Chariot of the Sun* which although peopled with baroque figures, and foreshortened in the baroque manner of the Calzi and the Palazzo Sandi, has none of the baroque heaviness. These figures melt deliciously into the atmosphere, luminous, bright, gay. Contemporary with these frescoes in the Palazzo Archinto was, very probably, the phantasy *Triumph of Zephyr and Flora* (No. 5), in which human bodies full of colour and sensuality are set against a background of the outspread gossamer wing of a dragonfly.

In the monumental *Story of Scipio and Sofonisba* (PL. 6 and 7) at the Palazzo Casati-Dugnani, Tiepolo returns to the Ricci-Veronese tradition and, in an orgy of light and harmonious colour, disposes a calvacade of elegant mannered youths and delicious, aristocratic-looking young girls, all dressed in the clothes of the sixteenth century, posed as it were, on the stage of a theatre, against a luminous back stage of renaissance arches and columns. This is his own particular brand of classicism. To satisfy the wishes of his rich clients, he clothed these figures in magnificent raiment, gave them noble attitudes, lordly gestures, all in the manner of the golden age of the sixteenth century, adapting himself particularly to the style of Veronese (another painter who knew how to pander to the tastes of the powerful ones of his time) and to Ricci's influence, so much so that he was considered their legitimate descendant, acclaimed after his work in the Palazzo Clerici as ' a Veronese raised from the dead '. Yet there is a considerable difference between the classicism of Tiepolo and that of Veronese. The earlier painter is more sedate, more measured, faithful to a precise climate of culture and costume; while Tiepolo's classicism is superficial, situated, it is true, among solemn facades and noble backgrounds, but peopled with seventeenth century men and women, Tiepolo's own contemporaries, in arcadian settings, festive, refined, part of the new age of roccoco. We must remember that sixteenth-century classicism and that of Tiepolo were separated by the baroque experience, as well as by the new roccoco style, and so when we say ' sixteenth-century classicism ', we mean something

PLATE 13 - FAITH - VILLA LOSCHI-ZILERI, BIRON ▶

PLATE 14 - THE VIRGIN IN GLORY, WITH SAINTS. DETAIL - PARISH CHURCH, ROVETTA

PLATE 15 - THE DANAIDES - UNIVERSITY MUSEUM, STOCKHOLM

PLATE 16 - ASCENT TO CALVARY - CHURCH OF SANT'ALVISE, VENICE

PLATE 17 - TELEMACHUS AND MENTOR - RIJKSMUSEUM, AMSTERDAM ▶

PLATE 18 - THE FAMILY OF DARIUS. DETAIL - VILLA CORDELLINA, MONTECCHIO

PLATE 19 - MAGNANIMITY OF SCIPIO. DETAIL - VILLA CORDELLINA, MONTECCHIO

PLATE 20 - MAGNANIMITY OF SCIPIO. SKETCH - NATIONAL MUSEUM, STOCKHOLM

very different from Tiepolo's brand, which is all nervous grace, full of musical overtones, gentler, more melancholy and disenchanted. Tiepolo's manner, with his love of the delicately sensual, the fleshy tints and comely limbs, the mythological subjects and sumptuous scenes, is very far from the smooth, rational harmonies of the academic hothouse world of the neo-classicists.

In 1732, we find him back again in Venice, engaged on a new kind of work. In Milan, we saw him impetuously painting walls and ceilings in a kind of spectacular theatre of form and colour; but here he returns to the easel and gives expression to the religious side side of his character, painting subjects of a biblical nature and investing his canvases with a sense of family piety and intimacy. The *Adoration of the Child Jesus* (PL. 8) is now in the sacristy of St Mark's; *Abraham visited by the Angels*, and the *Appearance of the Angel to Agar and Ishmael* are in the Scuola Grande di S Rocco; and the *Education of the Virgin* is in the Chiesa della Fava. In this last painting, he shows his curly headed angels hovering again above paradisal landscapes. The human figures, depicted in *chiaroscuro*, have something of Piazzetta about them, caressed by his light and colours. A strong religious sense also pervades the *Communion of St Gerolamo* in the Gallery in Stockholm, and the *Death of St Gerolamo* in the Poldi-Pezzoli Museum in Milan. Here the painting is nervous and sensitive, in tender tones of ivory and mother of pearl, or shot through with bright rays of sunlight, illuminating and vibrating around the body of the saint.

The Venetian period was short. At the end of 1732, Tiepolo went to Bergamo, where in two working periods, until the end of 1733, he painted the frescoes *Allegorical Figures* and the *Stories of John the Baptist* (PL. 9 and 11), on the cupola, the walls and choir of the Colleoni Chapel. In the wide, airy space between heaven and earth, he moves his figures vigorously, with rapid tremulous brushwork, in clear tones, sharpened by his wide diffused light of day. Among the sketches for this is the beautiful *Beheading of John the Baptist,* now in the Stockholm Museum.

The brushwork is again rapid and spontaneous, and vibrant light breaks into the centre of the scene, playing over the human figures and draperies, in his familiar *chiaroscuro.*

The same luminous atmosphere, the same vivacious, crystalline colours, of the Bergamo work are to be seen in the Villa Loschi-Zileri at Biron near Vicenza, where he painted frescoes in the spring of 1734. He worked here feverishly, night and day, (as he relates himself to a friend) on a series of *Allegories* (PL. 12 and 13) all inspired by subjects from classical mythology.

In this year, for the parish church of Rovetta near Bergamo, he also painted the reredos of the *Virgin in Glory, Adored by the Apostles and the Saints,* a painting full of gaily tumultuous figures, in luminous colours. The light palpitates on the figures in the foreground, the whimpering angels and saints, bearing them up, as if they were weightless, into the background of the clouds. St Peter is most daringly drawn, in a dazzling mass of white light as he moves forward, stretching out his arms and brandishing his key. In this painting, Tiepolo conveys a marvellous feeling of airiness, in the well composed and deeply felt portrait, aided by dazzling colouring and fluent brushwork. In the liveliness of its human figures, this reredos is one of Tiepolo's most brilliant and successful works.

Towards 1740, at Verolanuova near Brescia, he painted two grandiose canvases for the parish church, one depicting *the Fall of the Manna,* the other the *Sacrifice of Melchisedech.* His wide open, serene skies pullulate with luminous angels, while on earth he paints his elegant, harmonious human figures. A return to the classical sixteenth century manner is evident here, (it was already foreshadowed at Biron), with his reference to Tintoretto, especially in the play of light and shade, accentuating the foreground with shadows and then retiring into the background with his luminous vibrating colours which depict a world without weight or substance.

Tintoretto's influence is to be seen again in the monumental tryptich of the *Passion of Jesus*, painted between 1738 and 1740 for the Church of St Alvise in Venice. Here, the technique is again sixteenth century, the brushwork extended and superimposed, while the scintillating colours of the frescoes are softened under a web of tonal veils. His religious feelings animate the picture, especially in the central part of the *Ascent to Calvary* (PL. 16), an excited and crowded scene, where the cross is prolonged in the half shadow of the foreground on to a bowed and livid Christ. The whole painting is dominated on the line of the hill by a threatening intoxicated mob. And among the closer witness of Our Lord's ascent, certain staring faces, of Rembrantesque power, blanched with sudden light, emphasise the drama and tragedy.

It was now that Tiepolo's commissions began to increase very greatly, and he was forced to paint at high pressure; nor were his constant journeyings from one place to another calculated to ease the pressure. In 1739, after several sessions, he completed the fresco of *The Glory of St Domenico* on the ceiling of the Church of the Jesuits in Venice. The central fresco, the *Institution of the Rosario*, is a marvel of daring, spread out across the sky. From base to ceiling, the perspective rises in architectural fashion, varied by the skilfully depicted human figures leaning out, starting with the mob of heretics on the large lower cornice, rising up to a symphonic crescendo of luminous colour below the white saint on the balustrade. In the clear and sunny sky above, rosy-faced angels are rotating around the Virgin who sits serenely on her throne among the clouds. It Tiepolo's architectural motives and foreshortened figures here have links with the tradition of the Veronese models (the Story of Esther and St Sebastian) here, out in this open pulsating sky, with its vivid diffused lighting, its blue and silvery tints, its harmonious composition, we have the authentic language of Tiepolo.

The verve he shows in the *Gesuati* is elaborated the following year, in 1740, when we find him at work on the ample ceiling of the Palazzo Clerici in Milan, painting an Apollo riding in a luminous chariot into an ethereal Olympian world, full of gods and goddesses, strangely combined with earthly beings, sensual human men and women, even animals. Never before had he created such an animated and joyful medley of celestial and human forms, such sensuality, such love of life — all clothed in the most scintillating harmonious colours.

His love of graceful and beautiful figures is seen again in the *Danaides* (PL. 15), in the Stockholm Museum; and in the enchanting small curly headed figure of *Telemachus and Mentor* (PL. 17) in the Rijks Museum in Amsterdam, a painting vibrating with all his silvery luminosity against the clear background of the sky.

The period which begins at the *Gesuati* and the Palazzo Clerici, and is followed by the triumphant frescoes of Würzburg (1751-1753) is one of Tiepolo's most productive and successful. He has now fully mastered his technique, and is able to achieve any effect he desires, from the heroic to the idyllic, from the joyous to the dramatic, from the sacred to the profane. Faithful to the demands of the refined hedonistic society of his time, he is a master above all in depicting those beautiful young female limbs which swim in a sea of colour and light. And this society showed its gratitude, describing him in 1739, when he was just over forty, as ' the most famous among the virtuosi ', loading him with commissions which gave him no respite, and vying with one another for his work. Thanks only to his precocious genius and vitality, was Tiepolo able to satisfy all these demands.

Between 1740 and 1743, he worked in the Scuola del Carmine in Venice, decorating the ceiling of the meeting room with a *Virgin in Glory*, and the walls with groups of *Virtues*. This admirable work,

PLATE 22 - THE MEETING OF ANTONY AND CLEOPATRA - COLLECTION P. ROTHSCHILD, PARIS

PLATE 23 - BANQUET OF ANTONY AND CLEOPATRA. SKETCH - STOCKHOLM
MUSEUM

PLATE 24 - NEPTUNE OFFERS VENICE THE RICHES OF THE SEA. DETAIL - DUCAL PALACE, VENICE

ANGEL - MUNICIPAL MUSEUM, TRIESTE ▶

FAMILY GROUP - HORNE MUSEUM, FLORENCE

perhaps his greatest achievement, reveals how he was able, without incongruity, to fit a serious religious subject into his luminous sensual world of enchantment and lifelike nature. The Virgin is depicted in a white silvery raiment which billows out behind the flight of a train of shining angels. The Virtues, in their gently undulating glowing clothes, seem borne up effortlessly into the air. Parts of this work, such as the *Innocence* with its eyelids lowered and its gaze resting on a dove, are of unsurpassed lyricism. The same can be said for his *Meekness* and the sheep in its silvery light; or of the graceful *Angel*, with its foamy veils floating among the sinners in purgatory. In this subtle and enchanting masterpiece, one feels again the excited personality of the painter, as if he were present himself. Although the sixteenth century atmosphere has associations with Veronese paintings in the College and Library of Venice, this is a completely new and original work of art. Once again, we see Tiepolo's classicism of the sixteenth century, but overlaid with the contemporary roccoco.

In 1743 Tiepolo worked in the Church of the Scalzi, not this time on the chapel ceiling, but on the immense central frescoe showing the miraculous flight of the *Santa Casa di Loreto*, held up amid a choir of pullulating angels, surmounted by the solitary Virgin and Child in a broad halo of light. What progress he has made since his first great work, the *Glory of St Teresa* of 1725! That great gulf of sky which he always incorporated in his work — and which is a most important element in the painting of the time — is now no longer half empty but has become an abyss of silvery light, filled with choirs of beautiful angels. This masterpiece was, alas, destroyed in 1915, but two sketches of it remain: one in the Gallery of the Accademia in Venice, the other in the Roseberry Collection in London. The second is more faithful to the original, which far surpassed them both, on accourt of its huge surface.

In 1743 he alsa painted the great reredos in Bergamo Cathedral, depicting the *Martyrdom of St John Bishop of the City*, a painting flooded with wide white light. In the autumn of the same year, he left Venice for Montecchio Maggiore (Vicenza) near the Castle of Romeo and Juliet, where he worked in the Villa Cordellina, on frescoes of the *Family of Darius* (PL. 18) and the *Magnanimity of Scipio* (PL. 19), a hectic period with orders pouring in, so that he had to work at a continuous high pressure. In a letter to his friend Count Algarotti (a well-known man of letters and lover of the arts, who was on friendly terms with most of European royalty and therefore a good publicist for Tiepolo in this cosmopolitan world), Tiepolo complained of the bad weather and the chattering of the guests, which prevented him from working with the necessary concentration. In these paintings, the spectacular stagecraft of Tiepolo, the background of arches and columns surrounded by floating standards and flags, the elegant female raiments, all immersed in a bright southern light, in vivid crystalline colours, is elaborated even further in the Paul Painting. Less ambitious than these are the two preparatory sketches, showing the *Magnanimity of Scipio* (PL. 20) and the *Family of Darius*, full of chromatic subtleties as well as of black and white gradations. The first is in the Stockholm Museum, the second in the Hermann Collection at Beverley Hills.

In the same manner recalling Veronese, Tiepolo painted the *Banquet of Anthony and Cleopatra*, in 1744 for Count Algarotti; it is now in the Melbourne Gallery. Between 1745 and 1750, he painted the silky *Allegory of the Spouses* for the Palazzo Corner-Mocenigo (now in the Contini Collection in Florence); and also for the Palazzo Barbaro (now in the Haberstock Collection in Berlin), together with other pictures including the stupendous group of *Tarquin and Lucrezia* (PL. 21) where the female figure is lit up with blazing light against a dark background. Lastly in the ballroom of the Palazzo Labia in Venice, where he worked with his good friend, the perspective painter Mengozzi-Colonna, in that astonishing ' machine ' of illusory landscape and architecture, he painted the *Story of Cleopatra*.

This is a feat of breathtaking virtuosity. A clear vibrating light reveals a facade animated by a quantity of human figures, all clustering around architraves and cornices, some of them ingeniously foreshortened to suit the perspective drawing. *The Meeting of Antony and Cleopatra* gives the illusion of a stage, with wings and backcloth, about which actors are strolling gracefully, or moving in pairs to minuet-like gestures.

There is a subtly malicious touch in the *Banquet of Cleopatra* where the roccoco atmosphere is evident. Fascinated with this Cleopatra theme Tiepolo then painted a series of small canvases on it, with the same delicacy of tone and chromatic combinations, of *Meetings* and *Banquets*, among which is the remarkable *Meeting of Antony and Cleopatra* in the Edinburgh Gallery and in the Rothschild Collection in Paris (PL. 22); and the *Banquet of Antony and Cleopatra* in the Stockholm Museum (PL. 23); also in the Alexander Collection in London.

In 1748 Tiepolo finished the reredos of the Church of the Jesuits — for which he had been commissioned in 1740 — with the *Dominican Saints*, a 'return' in some ways to plastic forms and heavier tactile colours. Between 1745 and 1750, he painted the canvas of the allegory of *Venice receiving from Neptune the riches of the Sea* (PL. 24), for the Palazzo Ducale in Venice. This is in the elaborate Court-Decorative manner, with tender mellow colouring. There can be no doubt that the inspiration for this picture came from the sixteenth century pageantry painters, specially from Paolo; but Tiepolo displays here a freshness, a flexibility, a vehemence, which are original to his work, again revealing as well as his marvellous adaptability, the inimitable world of his own forms and colours.

In these gorgeous scenes of beautiful human figures and gay colours, we have an image of contemporary society which could thus survey itself in a mirror. But along with this went another very different world, a spiritual world, compounded from Tiepolo's very sincere and religious faith.

Fertile as ever in delighsful gay and profane scenes during the second half of the decade, Tiepolo also painted deeply felt episodes from the Passion, in a series of small canvases: *The Prayer in the Orchard*, *The Crowning with Thorns*, in the Hamburg Kunsthalle, *The Last Supper* in the Louvre, and the *Crucifixion* in the Museum of St Louis. For the Church of the Apostles in Venice he painted the small reredos of *Santa Lucia* (PL. 25), full of religious conviction, in tender dreamy colours; the faces of the Saints and that of the page wearing his lace collar are exquisite. For the Church of St Agatha of Lenderina, he painted another canvas depicting the *Martyrdom of Saint Agatha* (PL. 28), now in the Berlin Museum, a composition full of his deep emotion and dramatic sense, in warm and mellow colours.

Two exceptional works in Tiepolo's figurative repertory belong to this period, the *Portrait of the Procurator Giovanni Querini* in the Querini-Stampalia Penacotec in Venice, and the *Consilium in Arena* in the Udine Museum. In the accepted sense of the word, Tiepolo's portraitist activity seems modest enough. In fact, the faces and figures in his frescoes are nearly all taken from life. There is for instance his own fresh self-portrait at Udine, where he is wearing sixteenth century clothes and the collar of Jacob, in the scene of *Rachel hiding the Idols*; there is his portrait of the Apothecary inside the oval in the *Crucifixion of Burano*; there is another self-portrait, (together with a portrait of his son, Domenico), inserted in the magestic *Allegory of Europe* in the residence at Würzberg; and a delightful family group interpolated in the *apotheosis of the Pisani* at Stra.

Among the formal portraits commissioned and painted, that of the Procurator is the only one which is unquestionably by his hand. Under the curve of an arch, on the bright red carpet stands the figure of the magistrate, foreshortened in the baroque manner. It is a harsh, biting portrait, the crude light falling on the face, picking out the aquiline imperious features, the character of the man

PLATE 25 - COMMUNION OF SANTA LUCIA. DETAIL - CHURCH OF THE APOSTLES, VENICE

PLATE 27 - THE MARRIAGE OF FREDERICK BARBAROSSA AND BEATRICE OF
BURGUNDY - THE CASTLE, WÜRZBURG

◀ PLATE 26 - OLYMPUS. DETAIL - THE CASTLE, WÜRZBURG

PLATE 28 - MARTYRDOM OF SAINT AGATHA - KAISER FRIEDRICH MUSEUM, BERLIN

PLATE 30 - PORTRAIT OF ANTONY RICCOBONO - ACCADEMIA DEI CONCORDI, ROVIGO

page 61 - PLATE 29 - SAINT OSWALD - CARRARA ACADEMY, BERGAMO

PLATE 31 - THE ADORATION OF
THE MAGI - ALTE PINAKOTHEK,
MUNICH

PLATE 32 - ABRAHAM AND LOT ARRIVE IN THE LAND OF BETHEL - COLLECTION CARANDINI, ROME

handled with the intensity of a Rembrandt. (The influence of Rembrandt on Tiepolo must have been considerable, through the prints then coming to Venice in considerable numbers). There is now a tendency in Tiepolo, to indulge increasingly in 'jokes' or phantasy, against the Apollonian painters, distorting reality, revealing even a certain bitterness, but also a power of judgment and a characterisation, as well as a capacity for most subtle penetration of character which surpasses his normal love for purely beautiful figures. Equally realistic and documentary is the *Consilium* whose theme had been given him by Count Antonio of Montegmacco, to commemorate the meeting of the Great Council of the Order of Malta which had, in 1748, elected the Count a *Cavaliere*. On the crowds thronging the sides of the hall, shafts of bright light are falling, creating a kind of slow motion effect as the physiognomies are individually, one by one, illuminated. This painting is presumably entirely the work of Tiepolo, although certain details which are handled with a realism not customary in our painter, might have been done in collaboration with his son Domenico.

The son was naturally most anxious to identify himself and his work with his father but, as we shall see clearly later at Würzburg and in the Tiepolos own villa at Zianigo and, above all, at the Valmarana in Vicenza, there is something bitter about the work of Domenico, a tendency to go into closer realistic detail, anti-classical almost, his work often verging on the caricature.

We have now arrived at the great Würzburg period. After lengthy negotiations, in the autumn of 1750, Tiepolo left for the small German principality, as a guest of the Prince-Bishop, Philip of Greiffenklau, for whose new Residence he frescoed the walls. His sons, Domenico aged twenty-three and Lorenzo aged fourteen, accompanied him. Both reception and hospitality during the stay were on a princely scale.

In the Great Hall of the Emperor, he painted again the marvellous illusory scenes he had painted for the Palazzo Labia in Venice, but in place of the classical architecture he had created there in collaboration with the perspective painter Mengozzi-Colonna, he here employs stucco arabesques, spiral columns, to create an exquisitely roccoco atmosphere. The same crowds are disposed on the same footlights of a theatre, but here their surroundings, are embellished by sumptuous draperies of gilded stucco hoisted up at the sides as if opening out on to a proscenium. Through these open draperies appear scenes of the *Marriage of Barbarossa* (PL. 27) and of the *Investiture of the Bishop Arnoldo*, proud aristocratic faces, and elegant figures in the gorgeous colours and clothes of the sixteenth century. On the ceiling, in the centre of a broad burning shy, Apollo escorts the bride down to Barbarossa in a chariot drawn by superb horses who race through the sky like white meteors. This fresco is an unrestrained feast of winged *putti*, angels with torches, joyful youths and divinely beautiful girls, and standards waving in the irridescent air. Here, among the architectural phantasies of Central European roccoco, Tiepolo's own phantasy and inventive genius finds its home. Here, he adapts decoration and architecture in a perfectly unified whole.

So delighted was the Prince with this work that he made Tiepolo fresco the ceiling of the great stairway as well, a surface of six hundred square metres! With the valuable assistance of his son, Tiepolo carried out this immense work between 1752 and 1753 (PL. 26). In a series of magnificent allegories flung out across the sky, he assembled all the regions of the earth, the sea and the winds, Olympus and Paradise, together with human beings, the Prince-Bishop himself, his architect and court dignitaries, a dazzling company acclaimed on the long trumpets of his angels. On the left, between Europe and Africa, Tiepolo has depicted himself on the wrinkled surface of a stucco shell, ecstatic, quivering with life, accompanied by his son Domenico. This is the most breath-taking intoxicating spectacle he ever painted.

As if this was not enough during the Würzburg period, he also painted a number of canvases, among them the great altar piece of the *Adoration of the Magi* (PL. 31) for the Church of Schwarzach (now in the Munich Pinakothek). This is in the sumptuous Veronese manner, full of exotic human figures, lit up by rays of light falling on the extravagant silks and stuffs, lingering on the bosom of the Virgin and the Child, lighting them up with delicate silvery irridescence.

He also painted two large altar pieces, *the Assumption,* and the Expulsion of the Rebel Angels, for the Palace Chapel; and in a melancholy Arcadian setting, a series of small canvases with the *Story of Armida and Rinaldo* inspired by the sensual poetry of Tasso — a theme which was dear to him and to which he was to return often, until he expressed it in the masterpieces of the Valmarana at Vicenza. Among these are the scenes of rustling silks in *Armida crowning Rinaldo* and in *Armida and Rinaldo before the Mirror* (New York, private collection), and, most beautiful of all, the *Armida and Rinaldo* of the Art Institute in Chicago, with its elegiac landscape and the languid, subtly malicious postures; the sketches of *Rinaldo in the Garden of Armida* in the Berlin Gallery, and of *Rinaldo abandoning Armida,* in the Cailleux Collection in Paris, a landscape full of sweet melancholy and carefully shaded tonalities.

Tiepolo's sons, especially Domenico, were of great assistance to him at Würzburg. Domenico, although conscious of his father's example, here began to display an original style of his own, a greater feeling for reality, a certain bitterness even and disenchantment, but all expressed still with his father's clear luminous technique. Belonging to this period, too, are some engravings and canvases of popular and biblical subjects, among which are two paintings now in the Carandini-Albertini Collection in Rome, of the *Story of Abraham and Lot arriving in the land of Bethel* (PL. 32).

Late in the autumn of 1753, after three years in Germany, the Tiepolos, loaded with honours and rewards returned to Venice. It was now, with the Würzburg earnings at the Prince-Bishop's Palace, that Tiepolo bought the Villa of Zianigo near Mestre, which Domenico was later to fresco with his acid buffooneries.

Between 1754 and 1755, we find Tiepolo working again in Venice for the Church of the Pietà on a large fresco exalting the cardinal virtues. In the centre of the ceiling, in a large oval which seems to rotate, giving the whole a spiral movement, is a silvery Virgin ascending, in a turbulence of dazzling wings, accompanied by the music of angel choirs and celestial orchestras, which expand over into a vast skyscape full of clouds of mother of pearl. The transparent and luminous colours, burning yellow, blue, rose and silver white are clear even in the shaded parts of this picture. Particularly striking is the base entablature, with its details of the lutists.

In 1757, Tiepolo was back in Vicenza, on the Berici hills, frescoing the Villa of Count Valmarana. He was again accompanied by his son Domenico, to whom he entrusted the decoration of almost all the guests' quarters; while he reserved the villa decorations for himself. In the *Sacrifice of Iphigenia* on the ' portego ' or portico, we find, among the familiar theatrical wings and columns, the elegant figures and fluttering standards of the Veronese Court-Decorative style; but in the other rooms, decorated with episodes taken from the *Iliad*, the *Aeneid*, *Orlando Furioso* and *Gerusalemme Liberata* (PL. 33 and 34), is something new. His technique of perspective is no longer tied to the architectural frames of the sixteenth century; it depicts instead figures which move into the walls on parallel lines, with emphasis in depth making use of the atmospheric play of light and the gradations of colour in a new way. New, above all, is the spirit which seems to hover over this enchanted scene. Almost everywhere is a sweet and delicate grace, a love of beautiful sensitive figures in an elegiac rhapsody to Youth.

At Valmarana, Tiepolo is still the familiar inventor we know, capable still of creating a world of his own, the wonderful figures and

PLATE 33 - RINALDO AND ARMIDA - COLLECTION CAILLEUX, PARIS

PLATE 36 - ANGELICA AND MEDORUS - VILLA VALMARANA, VICENZA

PLATE 37 - RINALDO AND ARMIDA - VILLA VALMARANA, VICENZA ▶

PLATE 38 - FIGURES AND ARCHITECTURE OF A CEILING. DETAIL - CA' REZZONICO, VENICE

PLATE 39 - ALLEGORY OF THE REZZONICO-SAVORGNAN. DETAIL - CA' REZZONICO, VENICE ▶

PLATE 40 - THE RAPE OF HELEN - COLLECTION BORLETTI, MILAN

grandiose colour orchestrations, spreading out his phantasy on the broadest of horizons, as at Würzburg. But he was already aged sixty, and it seems now that some more humane feeling, of a kind of subtle personal melancholy, begins to insinuate itself into his ideal world. The figures are stile constructed with the point of the brush, but with a new sensitivity; the light lingers more attentively on them, as if to bring about a human intimacy, while the colours are more tender and delicate. This greater insistence on the human side may perhaps be traced to the influence of his son, Domenico, who had painted the guest houses — particularly those of Ciarlatano, Diorama and Passeggiate — where a more earthy humour breaks in. Moreover, Tiepolo's open mind was always ready for something new and original; and the ironical, satirical, but always humane, attitude of his talented son must have attracted him particularly. The tendency now is to add a touch of hallucination, of the grotesque and the comic, to his normal world of monumental designs, delving more deeply into the essence of things; in the later Spanish period, when he was working in Madrid, we become increasingly aware of this.

But among the most exquisite and enchanting scenes painted here for the villa, are those of the *Story of Angelica and Medoro* (PL. 36) and *Rinaldo and Armida* (PL. 33 and 37) depicting the lovers in gently undulating countryside, painted in green, blue and white, while in the far distance the sky is red and rosy. But in the *Stanza dell'Olimpo* at the guest house, there is a return to the Apollonian Tiepolo, with his luminous troops of gods and goddesses, borne on foaming wings of the clouds, accompanied by the beautiful new bodies of the angels.

About this time Tiepolo also decorated the city hall (destroyed in 1945) for the Count of Valmarana with allegorical frescoes. Among these, is the remarkable and fantastic *Truth triumphing over Lies* where the aged artist seems to be groping for something new to say, as in the figure of *Error* and in the hastily drawn groups of the *Lie* and the *Calumny*. For the altar-piece in the parish church of Rampazzo, he painted *St Gaetano in Gloria,* a picture full of his feeling for religion, the Saint floating in the clear silvery light. For the altar piece of the parish church of Noventa Vicentina, he also painted *Santi Rocco a Sebastiano,* again rich in spiritual feeling, and with the beautifully modelled figure of the naked Saint.

On the occasion of the marriage of the Procurator Lodovico to the Countess Savorgnan in the renovated Palazzo Rezzonico, Tiepolo frescoed two ceilings, and in the lively *Wedding Allegory of Rezzonico-Savorgnan* (PL. 39), he again drove his aerial quadriga through the blazing skies as at Würzburg, carrying in it this time the happy bride, surrounded in a halo of laughing angels, doves, amoretti, and the fluttering of standards. Here, the figures seemed to overflow outside the fresco, giving an illusion of actually moving on the entablature, in a glow of burning, joyous colour. The foreground is also treated in a novel manner for Tiepolo; instead of painting it in dark colours, to contrast it with the rest of the picture, he gives it bright and vivid colours, softening the background delicately in rose and blue and silver tints which become more and more tenuous and subtle as they disappear slowly into the sky above. The following year, Tiepolo did the frescoes on the ceiling of the Church Della Purità at Udine — an *Assumption* in the old manner, full of fluttering wings and silks, in his clear silvery almost milky tones. In the same year 1759, he painted the altar piece of St Tecla for the Church of Santa Maria delle Grazie at Este, revealing again his religious feelings as in the earlier canvases at Rampazzo and Noventa. This work is full of rapid nervous brushwork, and the human figures are tremulous against a rural background, palpitating with the reflections from the sky, in sensitive tones of grey-blue, rose and mother of pearl.

Still joyfully inspired by the phantasies of his open skies and comely limbs, Tiepolo is back in 1761 at Verona, at work on the frescoes of the *Triumph of Hercules* for the ceiling of the Palazzo

Canossa. Once again the fiery stallions of Würzburg and of the Ca'
Rezzonico ride through the skies, accompanied by a triumphal aerial
pyramid of forms and bodies, anticipating in shape the tower of the
fortress he was later to paint for the royal palace of Madrid.

Commissions were pouring in from every part of Europe, and he
had to work so hard or so quickly as now. Between 1761 and 1762,
he worked in the Villa Pisani at Stra, on the picturesque banks of
the Brenta, where he frescoed the roof of the ballroom with the *Glo-
ries of the House of Pisani*, one of the most famous and noble Venetian families, which he greatly admired. It is another exuberant
and joyful work, executed with his old verve and enthusiasm, displaying the painter again in his element on the vast surfaces. Once
again, he spreads his huge luminous sky across the ceiling, assembling
the familiar repertory of beautiful limbs and bodies, of glowing angels
and amoretti, in the great architectural mis-en-scène, filled with troops
of musicians and soldiers, in a sea of sun, brilliance and dazzling
colour.

The allegorical figures of the *Four Parts of the World* are accompanied by Pestilence and Vice, while in the sky above enthroned
in the clouds sits the Virgin and the Virtues clad in transparent white,
acclaimed by the trumpeters in the Hall of Fame. Below, on the
left of the picture, are family portraits, probably drawn from life,
and a small group of mandoline players astride the cornice, the whole
conceived in his fresh, airy, silvery style.

In 1761, when orders and commissions were pouring in and he
was feverishly completing the Pisani frescoes in Stra, the invitation
from the King of Spain to go to Madrid and do the frescoes in the
throne room of the Royal Palace arrived. Believing that he could
paint these quickly, Tiepolo accepted and, as soon as he had finished the frescoes at Stra, he set off for Madrid with his sons Domenico
and Lorenzo, leaving his other son, the priest Giuseppe, in charge
of the family.

He set to work immediately, and between 1762 and 1764 painted the grandiose frescoes of the *Apotheosis of Spain* (PL. 42) in the throne room. Here are three hundred square metres of open radiant sky, in which he created with his inimitable verve and mastery, as if summarising all his past life, his harmonious world of beautiful girls, steeds and exotic animals, of waving standards and flags, columns and vessels, towers and thrones, surmounted by his delicious flight of angels, the colour scheme varying from brightest tones down to the most subtle in milky silvery tints. The fresco in the ceiling of the room of the halberdiers, the *Apotheosis of Aeneas*, was painted between 1764 and 1766, as was the ceiling in the Queen's room, the *Triumph of the Spanish Monarchy*, full of his beloved allegories, and gay with luminous colours. This was his last large scale painting, and with it ends the fabulous career as the greatest fresco painter the world has ever known.

When the ceilings were finished, he was invited to stay on in the service of the King. He accepted, but be soon became subject to jealousies and rivalries. The King supported him wholeheartedly, but secret intrigues among the courtiers and a group of 'neo-classicists', who were very influential at court, made his life difficult. Inspired by the rules of the stiff and archeological classicism of the German Winkelmann — so different from the fragrant, warm, luminous brand of Tiepolo — these men were headed by Mengs and Bayeu who dominated the Royal Academy of Fine Arts. In spite of this, he still painted enthusiastically, and much of this later work crossed the frontiers of Spain for the most distant parts of Europe. Among the Spanish pictures completed in this 1767 to 1769 period, are the seven altar pieces commissioned by the King for the Convent Church of Aranjuez, illustrating subjects selected by Father Giovacchino da Electa, a most influential man at court, where he was royal confessor and among the bitterest adversaries of our Italian painter. This man supported the neo-classicist completely, to the point

PLATE 4I - THE MADNESS OF ULYSSES - COLLECTION BORLETTI, MILAN

PLATE 42 - APOTHEOSIS OF THE SPANISH MONARCHY. DETAIL OF THE SPANISH
PROVINCES ROYAL PALACE, MADRID

PLATE 43 - CHRIST CALMS THE TEMPEST - COLLECTION G. FODOR, PARIS

VENUS AND MARS - HORNE MUSEUM, FLORENCE

◀ PLATE 44 - THE DEPOSITION - PRIVATE COLLECTION, ZURICH

A GENTLEMAN - CORRER
MUSEUM, VENICE

BUFFOONS - MUNICIPAL
MUSEUM, TRIESTE ▶

of having Tiepolo's altar pieces removed and replaced by those of his friends. Of these altar pieces, which were long dispersed all over Spain and then collected (in part altered), in the Prado and the Royal Palace in Madrid, and in European and American collections elsewhere, four sketches are conserved — in the Seilern collection in London — representing St Pasquale Baylau, St Francis of Assisi, St Carlo Borromeo and St Giuseppe, all pervaded with Tiepolo's profound mystical-religious sentiment, the figures rendered with impetuous loose brushwork, nervously drawn, vibrating with his clear, delicately shaded silvery tones. Here too we see landscapes drawn from nature, arid and stony scenes from the harsh Madrid plateau, invested with a feeling of sadness, even anguish, very far from Tiepolo's tender, familiar, intimate landscapes of the Valmarina. Among these dramatic scenes are the *Deposition* in the Pinto — Barto Collection of Lisbon, the figures around the Cross bathed in livid light, with gulfs of shadow in the background; the *Flight into Egypt* from the same collection, with a small group of fugitives in the barque, surmounted by a white shining angel on the dark mountainside; the *Rest during the Flight into Egypt* in the same collection, with extremely small dark figures against the light, again surmounted by a high and overhanging rock; the *Quietening of the Tempest* (PL. 43) in the Fodor Collection in Paris, the elements wind and rain depicted in vivid chiaroscuro, while the figure of Christ is set agaínts a background of the white sail. Lastly the *Deposition from the Cross* (PL. 44) in Zurich (private collection) full of sorrowful gestures, while the light breaks in on the figures in the foreground and the livid crosses rise dramatically behind, re-echoing the line of the distant landscape. No painting could be more intensely ' felt ' than this, with its mastesly drawing and design, marvellously alive, as the light falls on the human forms animating them dramatically.

The young Goya, then an enthusiastic apprentice to the arts, must surely have seen these paintings. It was the great Venetian, the great foreign artist, who fascinated him and started the ferment destined to express itself with burning Spanish ardour. It was the Tiepolo wide skies opening out on to infinite horizons, intoxicating with their sunlight, their warm, harmonious, human figures, physically beautiful yet always human, Tiepolo's sincere and profound religion, his imaginative design, more than the Spaniards neo-classical fellow countrymen with their lifeless world of archeological research, which influenced Goya.

Giambattista Tiepolo died unexpectedly, on the 27th of March 1770, at the age of seventy-four. Of his earthly remains nothing is conserved, for the Madrilena Church which held them was later destroyed. But for those who seek delight and consolation in the beauty and poetry of life, something more imperishable remains, to testify to the many sided genius of this divine artist.

GIAMBATTISTA TIEPOLO
(chronological details)

1696, born probably the 5th March, in Venice, in Corte S Domenico in the parish of S Pietro di Castello. The son of Domenico, ship proprietor (the Venetian term *Parcenevole di vascello*) and of Orsetta Giogali.

1697, Tiepolo and his five young brothers lose their father. Inherit a modest patrimony.

1715-1716, in the arch interstices of Santa Maria dei Derelitti (called the Ospedaletto) in Venice, paints the *Sacrifice of Isaac*, considered his first work (Da Canal, 1732).

1716, enters a competition with other painters (Da Canal 1732). On the saint's day of St Rocco he exhibits in public in front of the Church and the School of the same name, as was customary, a *Faraone sommerso*. The work was widely acclaimed. Today it is lost (Da Canal, 1732).

1717, he joins the ' *fraglia* ' or fraternity of Venetian painters. This must mean that he had finished his apprenticeship with Gregorio Lazzarini, his first master (Da Canal, 1732).

1717-1719. He paints the *Ripudio di Agar*, his first signed and dated work. It is now in the Rasini Collection in Milan.

1719, 21 November. Marries the seventeen year old Cecilia Guardi, sister of the painters Antonio and Francesco Guardi. From this happy marriage he had nine children. Among them Domenico and Lorenzo who were to become painters themselves and valuable collaborators with their father.

1721 approx. In competition with the most popular painters of the time, as five years before at the Ospedaletto, he paints for the City church of St Stae the *Martirio di S Bartolomeo*, part of a series of twelve canvases depicting ' Scenes from the life of the Apostle ' (Da Canal, 1732).

1721-1722 approx. For the Capella dei Carmelitani in the Venetian church of St Aponal he paints the *Madonna del Carmelo con Santi e anime purganti* (Da Canal, 1732). Now in the Brera Pinacotec in Milan.

1722. The Doge Cornaro, for who mTiepolo had painted, dies. In his

Palace (now Mocenigo Palace) and at St Polo, he paints paintings and portraits (lost) and superintends, ' organisation of pictorial matters ' (Da Canal, 1732).

1725. About this time he does the frescoes in the Church Chiesa degli Scalzi in Venice, the Cappella di di S Teresa, entitled *Gloria della Santa*. The Bolognese painter, Mengozzi-Colonna, collaborates in the architectural-ornament part of the painting. Works with Tiepolo until 1762. In the Venetian Palace dei Sandi, in Corte dell'Albero, paints the ceiling fresco of *Allegoria dell'Eloquenza* and other canvases to decorate the walls of the great hall (now in the possession of the Conte da Schio at Castelgomberto Vicentino).

1725. Still in Venice, executes for the principal room of the Palazzo Dolfin at S. Pantalon a series of ten large canvases with the *Episodi di Storia Romana*.

1725. He paints at Udine in the Palazzo dell'Arcivescovo Dionigi Dolfin, a member of the Venetian family, the ceiling of the big staircase, *La Cacciata degli Angeli Ribelli*. ' A stairway of this kind is not to be found in all Italy ', said a certain priest, Gioseffo, in a letter to a friend, dated the 30th July 1725. Udine.

1726. Still at Udine, paints the fresco of the Cappella del SS. Sacramento, in the Cathedral. In the document commissioning this work is described as ' the celebrated and lucid painter '. Continues to do the frescoes in the Archbishop's Palace, painting: in the gallery *l'Angelo annunciante a Sara la sua maternità, Rachele che nasconde gli idoli, l'Apparizione degli Angeli ad Abramo;* in three ovals on the ceiling: *il Sacrificio d'Isacco, Agar nel deserto* and *il Sogno di Giacobbe;* in the ' Red Room ' the Giudizio di Salomone. Informed recent criticism definitely rejects the theory that in these cycle of frescoes the artist obtained help.

1731. At Milan, in the Palazzo Archinto, paints the frescoes for the ceiling of the great hall with *Trionfo delle Arti*, and other ceilings, with *Fetonte che chiede ad Apollo di guidare il carro del sole, Perseo che rapisce Andromeda, Giunone con la Fortuna e Venere.* In 1943 this Palazzo was destroyed during an aerial bombardment. In the Palazzo Casati in Milan now the Dugnani Palace, paints the frescoes in the principal room, with the *Allegoria della Magnanimità* on the ceiling, and on the walls three episodes from Roman history; *Sofonisba che riceve il veleno inviatole da Massinissa,* the *Generosità di Scipione* and *Scipione e lo schiavo.* In September is invited to Bergamo to paint the frescoes in the Cappella Colleoni.

1732. ' In the last months ' his painting the *Adorazione del Bambino Gesù* (Zanetti, 1733) is placed in the Church of St Giuliano, the Vicar's Church of the Venetian Basilica of St Marco. Is is now in the sacristy of the Canons of St Mark.

1732-1733. Returns to Bergamo, where he completes the decoration of the Cappella Colleoni with frescoes depicting *Storie del Battiste*.

1734. At Biron, near Vicenza, paints the frescoes in the Villa Loschi-Zileri, with *Figurazioni allegoriche* on the ceiling, on the walls of the main hall, and on the great stairway. This undertaking is commemorated in the building by a plaque. Confirmed by the artist himself, in a letter to Lodovico Feronati, dated the 10th April 1734, in which he says that he has been ' three months in Vicenza for a considerable undertaking '. For the Parish Church of Rovetta (Bergamo) dedicated to all the saints, paints the reredos, with the *Vergine in gloria adorata da Apostoli e Santi;* two years afterwards placed on the altar.

1735-1740. Paints the two huge canvases for the parish church of Verolanuova (Brescia) depicting the *Caduta della Manna,* and the *Sacrificio di Melchisedech,* probably commissioned by Count Gian Francesco Gambara, the local mayor.

1736. He fails to agree with the Conte de Tessin, the Swedish Minister in Venice, about payment for the decorations in the new Royal Palace of Stockholm; does not accept the invitation to go there. In the same year, the Count sends certain of his works (among which the *Danae*) to the Superintendent of

the Palace. They are now in the museum of the university.

1737. Paints the frescoes in the church of S Ambrogio, Milan; the chapel of S Vittore, of the *Decollazione* of S Vittore and the *Naufragio di S Satiro*. In Venice, agrees on the contract for the frescoes of the ceiling in the church of Santa Maria del Rosario ai Gesuati. To be completed by October of 1939.

1739. Invited by the Council of the Scuola del Carmine in Venice to decorate the ceiling of the Hall of Audience. In the relevant documents dated the 21st December 1739, is described as ' the most celebrated of all the virtuosi '. The whole work to be completed by 1744.

1740. Commissioned to paint a tryptich of the Passion of Christ for the Venetian church of S Alvise. This is mentioned in the ' Forestiere Illuminato ' in September '40, referring to his *Calvario*. At Milan, in the palace of the Marchese Giorgio Antonio Clerici, a marshal in the Court of Maria Teresa of Austria, paints the frescoes for the vault of the gallery with the *Corsa del Sole nell'Olimpo ed Allegorie delle quattro Parti del Mondo*.

1743. For the Cathedral of Bergamo paints the reredos with the Martyrdom of *S Giovanni Vescovo della Città*. At Montecchio Maggiore (Vicenza), in the Villa Cordelina, paints the frescoes for the ceiling of the great hall, with the *Allegoria della Nobiltà e delle Virtù* (now conserved in the town museum of Vicenza). In a letter to his friend Conte Algarotti dated 26th October 1743, referring to the progress of this work, expresses himself indignantly, ' I am here, yet unable to do anything, on account of the many strangers here '. The frescoes on the walls were probably finished in the following year — la Generosità di Scipione and the Famiglia di Dario davanti ad Alessandro.

1743-1744. In the Church of Santa Maria di Nazareth degli Scalzi in Venice paints the frescoes for the ceiling (destroyed during the Austrian bombardaments of 1915) — the Trasporto della Santa Casa di Loreto.

1744-1745. Paints on canvas, for a ceiling in the Palazzo Barbarigo in Venice, the Fortezza e la Sapienza. This painting was transported in 1936 into the city collection, in the Ca' Rezzonico in Venice.

1745-1750. Paints on canvas for the ceiling of the hall of the Fasti in the Venetian Palace of the Barbaro at S Stefano, the Apoteosi di Francesco Barbaro (now in the Metropolitan Museum of New York); and for the doors, four ovals, with the Offerta dei doni a Cleopatra (now in the Museum of Atlanta, U.S.A.); the Timoclea e il comandante (now in the National Gallery of Washington); the Tarquinio e Lucrezia, (now in the Haberstock Collection of Berlin); and the Fidanzamento (now in the Museum of Copenhagen). While in Venice, paints for the Palazzo Corner-Mocenigo, l'Allegoria degli Sposi di Casa Cornaro (now in the Contini Collection in Florence). Commissioned by the Conte Antonio de Montegnacco, the Canon of Quileia, in precise and detailed terms, to paint the Consilium in Arena (now in the Museum of Udine), in memory of the election of this nobleman and his friend, Count Florio, to the Order of Malta. In collaboration with the perspective painter Mengozzi-Colonna, decorates the central room of the Palazzo Labia, with frescoes on the ceiling depicting the Genio su Pegaso che mette in fuga il tempo; and the walls, with l'Incontro di Antonio e Cleopatra and the Banchetto di Cleopatra.

1750. On the 12th December, arrives with his sons, Domenico and Lorenzo, in Würzburg in Franconia, to decorate the new residential palace of the Prince-Bishop, Carlo Filippo di Greiffenklau. In the Imperial room paints the frescoes on the ceiling, Apollo che conduce al Barbarossa la sposa Beatrice di Borgogna; and on the walls, the Nozze del Barbarossa con Beatrice di Borgogna, and the Investitura del Vescovo Aroldo a Vescovo di Würzburg. The whole completed in 1752. In the same year, commissioned to paint the frescoes for the ceiling of the monumental staircase. In 1953, completes the following paintings: at the top l'Olimpo, and at the sides, the Allegorie dell'Europa, dell'Asia, dell'Africa e dell'America.

1753. While in Würzburg, paints the altar

piece of the *Adorazione dei Magi* (now in the old Pinakothek of Munich), for the Church of the Benedettini di Schwarzach.

8th November 1753: the Tiepolo family start their return to Venice.

1754. At Nervesa (Treviso), probably with the help of his son, Domenico, paints several monochromes in the Villa Volpato-Panigai (now in the Berlin Painting Gallery). Simultaneously, in Nervesa, decorates with the help of other painters, the Villa Soderini-Berti. These frescoes, among which is the famous *l'Apoteosi della Famiglia Soderini*, were destroyed during the First World War, in 1917.

1754-1755. Paints the frescoes for the ceiling of the Church della Purità in Venice, the *Trionfo della Fede*.

1755-1756. At Mira (Venice), along the banks of the Brenta canal, in collaboration with the perspective painter Mengozzi-Colonna, paints for the principal room of the Villa Contarini, the *Ricevimento del Re Enrico III di Francia*, an event which had taken place in 1574. This fresco was later removed, and is now in the Jacquemart-André Museum in Paris.

1756. The Venetian Academy of Painting and Sculpture elects him President.

1757. At Vicenza, paints, with the help of his son, Domenico the frescoes in the Villa dei Conti Valmarana and the guest annexe: *Episodi dell'Illiade, dell'Eneide, dell'Orlando Furioso e della Gerusalemme Liberata*, and *Figurazioni mitologiche*

e allegoriche, and *Scene popolari e carnevalesche*. Thanks to the recently discovered, clear interpretation of the date of these paintings, by the son, 1757 — and not 1737 as was previously supposed — it has been possible to establish definitively most of the dates of Tiepolo's paintings. (Morassi, 1943).

While in Vicenza, also paints the frescoes for the ceiling of the great reception room of the Palazzo Trento-Valmarana, (destroyed by aerial bombardment in 1945): the *Trionfo della Verità sopra la Menzogna*.

1758. Venice. In the renovated Palazzo dei Rezzonico on the Grand Canal, paints the frescoes for two ceilings, the *Allegoria del Merito tra la Nobiltà e la Virtù* and the *Allegoria nuziale*, both to commemorate the marriage between the Rezzonico and Savorgnan families.

1759. Udine. Between the 14th August and 16th September, paints the frescoes for the ceiling of the Cappella della Purità, an *Assunta*. On Christmas eve at Este, his large altar piece the *S Tecla che implora per la liberazione della città dalla peste* was placed on the great altar in the Cathedral.

1761. Verona. In conjunction with the Milanese decorator Visconti paints the frescoes for the ceiling of the Palazzo Canossa, the *Trionfo d'Ercole*.

1761-1762. Stra (Venice). On the Brenta Canal, not far from Mira, paints the frescoes for the huge ceiling in the ballroom of the Villa Pisani, *Glorie di Casa Pisani*. In the spring of the same year, completes the arrangements with King Charles III of Spain to decorate the throne room of his palace and, together with his sons, Domenico and Lorenzo, leaves for Madrid. Arrives in Madrid on 2nd June. Is indisposed for some time, and stays with the Venetian ambassador.

1762-1767. Paints the frescoes for the ceiling of the throne room, the *Apoteosi della Spagna;* the ceiling of the Sala degli Alabardieri, *Enea condotto al Tempio dell'Immortalità da Venere;* and the ceiling of the Queen's ante-chamber, the *Trionfo della Monarchia spagnola*. The two last with the help of his sons. This series of paintings completed, is invited by the King to stay on and work in Madrid. Accepts the invitation.

1767-1769. On the instructions of the King, and advice of the architect Sabbatini, paints seven large high altars for the new church of S Pasquale di Aranjuez. The subjects of these paintings were suggested by Padre Gioacchino de Electa, the King's confessor, a most influential courtier, and at the same time, a bitter enemy of Tiepolo. These altar pieces were replaced by others, and dispersed throughout Spain after Tiepolo death, owing to the personal feud with Padre Gioacchino. They have fortunately been found again.

1770. 27th March. Tiepolo dies unexpectedly, at the age of seventy four. Buried in the Chiesa Madrilena di S Martino, which was later destroyed, and no trace of his remains exist today. His son Domenico returns to Venice. Lorenzo remains in Spain where after a few years, he dies.

LIST OF PLATES

LIST OF DRAWINGS

REPRODUCTIONS PRINTING AND BINDING EXECUTED
BY THE ISTITUTO ITALIANO D'ARTI GRAFICHE OF
BERGAMO (ITALY)